Reducing Your Tax Bill

Time-saving books that teach specific skills to busy people, focusing on what really matters; the things that make a difference – the *essentials*.

Other books in the series include:

Making Your Money Grow

Managing Your Money

Planning Your Retirement

Making a Will

Create Great Spreadsheets

Accounting for the Small Business

Making the Most of Your Time

For full details please send for a free copy of the latest catalogue.
See back cover for address.

Reducing Your Tax Bill

John Claxton

ESSENTIALS

To Emily and Aidan

Published in 2001 by
How To Books Ltd, 3 Newtec Place,
Magdalen Road, Oxford OX4 1RE, United Kingdom
Tel: (01865) 793806   Fax: (01865) 248780
e-mail: info@howtobooks.co.uk
www.howtobooks.co.uk

All rights reserved. No part of this work may be reproduced or stored
in an information retrieval system (other than for purposes of review),
without the express permission of the publisher in writing.

© **Copyright 2001 How To Books Ltd**

British Library Cataloguing in Publication Data.
A catalogue record for this book is available from
the British Library.

Edited by Diana Brueton
Cover design by Shireen Nathoo Design
Produced for How To Books by Deer Park Productions
Typeset by PDQ Typesetting, Newcastle-under-Lyme, Staffordshire
Printed and bound in Great Britain by Bell & Bain Ltd., Glasgow

NOTE: The material contained in this book is set out in good faith for
general guidance and no liability can be accepted for loss or expense
incurred as a result of relying in particular circumstances on
statements made in the book. Laws and regulations are complex
and liable to change, and readers should check the current position
with the relevant authorities before making personal arrangements.

ESSENTIALS *is an imprint of*
How To Books

Contents

Preface		**7**
1	**Income Tax Rules**	**9**
	Allowances, reliefs and rates	10
	Credits	18
	Investment income	21
	Employees	23
	Self-employed	27
	Self-assessment	28
2	**Income Tax Planning**	**32**
	Tax-free benefits-in-kind	34
	Taxable benefits-in-kind	36
	Spouses	37
	Children	40
	Loss-making businesses	41
	Annual planning	42
3	**National Insurance Contributions**	**45**
	Employee contributions class 1	47
	Self-employed contributions (classes 2 and 4)	48
	Voluntary contributions (class 3)	49
	Planning	49
4	**Capital Gains Tax**	**52**
	Taxable gains and losses	54

	Indexation	55
	Taper relief	57
	Calculating the gain	60
	Reliefs	62
	Planning	65
5	**Inheritance Tax**	**69**
	Exempt lifetime transfers	71
	Potentially exempt and immediately chargeable transfers and taper relief	73
	Investments free of IHT	75
	Calculating the inheritance tax payable	76
	Planning	78
	Deeds of variation	84

Appendix A Example of the extra age and married couples' allowances for pensioners	87
Appendix B Example of a taxable capital gains calculation on shares	90
Appendix C Example of how immediately chargeable transfers, potentially exempt transfers and IHT taper relief work	93

Preface

If you think you are paying too much tax (and who does not!) this is the book for you.

One of the best ways of saving money is not spending it, and not spending it on tax, for which there is no return at all, must be worth following up.

When did you last look at:

~ the income tax allowances, to make sure you are getting your share

~ your National Insurance contributions – they are a tax, too

~ avoiding capital gains tax liability

~ making sure your heirs do not get clobbered for inheritance tax.

It is really not very difficult to arrange your affairs so that the tax man gets no more than a fair share of your income and wealth.

Note: many tax numbers change every year in the budget. Some of the rules get changed too. Throughout this book the rules and numbers used are those relevant to the tax year 2001/2002.

John Claxton

1 Income Tax Rules

Before you can plan to reduce your income tax bill you need to understand the rules.

In this chapter, six things that really matter:
- ~ Allowances, reliefs and rates
- ~ Credits
- ~ Investment income
- ~ Employees
- ~ Self-employed
- ~ Self-assessment

Everyone says the income tax rules are complicated but, if rewritten in plain English and approached gently, they can be understood. There are many areas where you can reduce your liability, if you know about them.

It has become worse for the self-employed and for certain employees with complicated affairs, due to the need to complete self-assessment forms. With a bit of effort they can be managed but if your affairs are very involved it is worth considering employing an accountant to do it for you, at least for the first time.*

Is this you?

I am sure I am paying too much income tax but the rules are so mystifying. • I would like to know if I get any additional allowances on retirement. • Am I entitled to any of these new tax credits? • I have expenses related to work – can they be set against my income for tax purposes? • I would make more pension contributions if I knew they would be tax free. • I have to fill in self-assessment forms and they are so complicated.

Allowances, reliefs and rates

Allowances are amounts which can be set against your income each year to reduce the amount of income tax payable. Reliefs arise in respect of certain payments that you make,

* Remember that it is not the job of the Inland Revenue to suggest to you ways of saving tax – after all, they do not know your circumstances. It is up to you.

such as pension scheme contributions, and are deducted from income in arriving at taxable income.

Allowances and reliefs tend to be varied each year in the budget, usually by an adjustment to take account of inflation, but sometimes by more – or less !

After deducting your allowances and reliefs, what is left is taxable income and is subject to tax at increasing rates for successive bands of annual taxable income:

~ Lower rate band   10% up to £1,880
~ Basic rate band   22% £1,881 to £29,400
~ Higher rate band 40% over £29,400

The bands tend to be increased each year in line with inflation. The rates are changed from time to time.

Personal allowance

The personal allowance of £4,535 is available to everyone with income, including children. It has the effect of reducing your tax bill at the highest rate of tax being paid by you.

The personal allowance is increased in the year you reach the age of 65 and again on reaching 75, subject to an income limit, as follows:

~ age allowance age 65–74: £5,990
~ age allowance age 75 and over: £6,260
~ income limit for age allowance: £17,600

Above the limit the extra age allowance is cut back on the basis of £1 for every £2 above, so that it reduces to £4,535 when income reaches £20,510 for those between 65 and 74, and £21,050 for those aged 75 and over.

Married couples' allowance (MCA)

The MCA was abolished from 6 April 2000 except for couples where one partner at least was 65 or over on 6 April 2000, i.e. was born before 6 April 1935 but not for those born later, even when they reach 65.

The MCA for over 65s is £5,365 and for over 75s £5,435 but is subject to the same income limit and rate of cutback as the personal allowance, to a minimum of £2,070.

The reduction only takes place after the personal allowance has been fully cut back (see above).

The MCA is limited to 10% and so only reduces the tax bill by that percentage of the allowance.

The husband normally gets the MCA. A husband and wife can jointly decide that the wife will get it or that it be split equally between them, but it can go to the wife only if the husband has insufficient income to use it, not if the husband's income exceeds maximum cut-back figures.*

Blind person's allowance

You must be a registered blind person to receive this £1,400 allowance. If you are unable to use all of it the unused balance can be transferred to your spouse.

Interest on loans

Mortgage interest relief was abolished from 6 April 2000. However you can claim tax relief on certain other loans, such as to buy or improve a property you rent or to buy a car

See Appendix A for an example of the extra age and married couples' allowances for pensioners.

for use in your job, although this excludes travelling from home to work.

Pension scheme contributions

Reliefs are available against earned income for contributions you make to occupational or personal pension schemes, subject to certain limits expressed as percentages of pay.

The relief for occupational scheme contributions (including additional voluntary contributions) is limited to 15% of salary and there is a maximum salary to which it applies, currently £95,400.

For personal pensions there is no salary limit and the contribution limits are related to age at the start of the tax year, as follows:

- under 36   17.5%
- 36 to 45   20%
- 46 to 50   25%
- 51 to 55   30%
- 56 to 60   35%
- 61 and over   40%

Now that stakeholder pensions have started it

Income Tax Rules 15

is possible to make annual contributions of £3,600 to personal or stakeholder pensions, or both together, the earnings-related limits only applying to higher levels of contributions.

In this case the Inland Revenue adds a tax rebate to your contributions equivalent to the standard rate of tax (i.e. currently just over 28p for each £1) even if you pay no tax. Higher rate taxpayers can claim back the balance at the year-end.

Expenses at work

If you are employed and you have to pay for things you use at work, such as tools or working clothes, or for travelling expenses (but not from home to work), or for subscriptions to professional bodies, you can get relief.*

* The amount of relief may have already been agreed with the Inland Revenue by your trade union or employer.

Mileage allowances

The Inland Revenue has authorised mileage rates for use of an employee's car on company business, which may therefore be paid free of income tax. Payments in excess of these amounts will be taxable.

The current amounts are:

Engine size	Each mile	
	first 4,000	over 4,000
Up to 1,500cc	40p	25p
1,501 – 2,000cc	45p	25p
over 2,000cc	63p	36p

The allowance changes from April 2002 to one are based on mileage – 40p per mile for the first 10,000 miles in the tax year, 25p per mile thereafter.*

Self-employed taxpayers whose turnover does not exceed the VAT threshold (currently £54,000) can use these rates as an alternative to keeping detailed records of actual expenditure.

Rent-a-room

This is a special rule which applies if you rent out furnished accommodation in your only or main home. If you receive less than (currently) £4,250 a year gross income, i.e.

If you use your bicycle for business, your employer can pay you up to 20p per mile.

before deducting expenses, it is tax free. This is called Method A.

If your gross income is above the maximum, you have the choice of taking the first £4,250 tax free and paying tax on the rest, or being able to deduct expenses from the gross income and paying tax on the whole of the net amount (Method B). You can change from one method to the other as often as you wish, subject to notification to your Tax Office.

The rule applies even if your home is rented rather than owned by you (but you need to check whether your lease allows you to take in a lodger). It also applies if part of the income is for services, such as meals and laundry, but you cannot deduct expenses from the gross amount in the case of Method A.

Maintenance payments

Pensioners still entitled by age to the married couples' allowance get relief on maintenance payments, subject to the same income limit and rate of cutback.

Backing films

Relief from income tax is available for film production costs as long as the total costs are less than £15 million and are at least 70% insured in the UK.

Charitable payments

Every payment to a charity now qualifies for recovery by the charity of the tax deducted. If you are a higher rate taxpayer, you receive a tax rebate for the additional amount of tax.*

Credits

Tax credits have replaced certain National Insurance benefits. They are applied for on forms available from Benefits Agency offices, Job Centres, Post Offices and Tax Enquiry Centres, as well as Citizens' Advice Bureaux.

Working families' tax credit

This replaces family credit for couples (or single parents) with one or more children living with them. One parent must be working for at least 16 hours a week and

---

* Make sure you are receiving all the allowances and reliefs you are entitled to.

savings cannot be more than £8,000.
There are four parts:

~ A basic tax credit of £53.15 a week.*

~ A further amount of £11.25 if the main earner works for more than 30 hours a week.

~ Additional payments for each child depending on the age of the child:
  - 0–15 £25.60
  - 16–18 £26.35

~ A childcare tax credit of up to 70% of eligible child care costs up to a ceiling of £135 a week for one child and £200 for two or more. 'Eligible' in this case normally means registered child carers.

~ A disabled child tax credit of an additional £22.25 a week for each child who receives Disability Living Allowance or is registered blind.

This increases by £5 a week in June 2001.

For every £1 of net family income above £91.45 a week, 55p of the total credit is withdrawn.

Disabled person's tax credit

This replaces the disability working allowance. The disabled person must be working for at least 16 hours a week and savings cannot be more than £16,000.

The weekly amount of credit is £55.15 for a single person or £84.90 for a couple. (These amounts increase by £5 a week in June 2001.)

The same amounts for working for at least 30 hours a week, and for children and childcare, and the same withdrawal rules apply as for the working families' tax credit, except that the threshold for withdrawals is £71.10 for single persons.

Children's tax credit

Despite the name this new arrangement is not a credit at all but an allowance. It is available to all families with one or more children under 16 living with them. Income tax relief is given at 10% on £5,200, reducing the tax bill of eligible families by £520.*

* Next year the amount on which the 10% credit is calculated will be doubled to £10,400 for the first year of a baby born after 5 April 2002.

Either parent can claim it, but if the one claiming it is liable to tax at the higher rate, £1 of tax credit will be lost for every £15 of income in the 40% band. This means that the credit starts to be cut back when the relevant income exceeds £33,900 and it is completely lost when it reaches £50,000.

Investment income

Investment income is taxed at 20% unless total taxable income for the year enters the 40% band. Then a further 20% is payable on any investment income in that band.

If total income for the year is below the 22% band, investment income is taxed at 10% and if below the 10% band is tax free. Tax deducted at source at 20% can be recovered.

Investment income is treated as the top slice of income, so that the allowances and lower rate bands are used against earned income first. 'Top-slicing relief' is a term used to describe how higher-rate tax is applied to investments where the income becomes subject to higher-rate tax at the end of the investment period (with-profits bonds, for example).

The total taxable income for the period is divided by the number of years the money has been invested and the resultant amount is added to your income for the final year. If any or all of it falls into the higher-rate band, a further 18% is payable on that amount multiplied by the number of years.

Tax is deducted from bank and building society interest at the rate of 20% before it is paid, unless recipients have completed a form (obtainable from the bank or building society) saying that their total income is below their total allowances.

Dividends on shares are treated as having been taxed at source at 10% (this is sometimes called the dividend tax credit). It cannot be avoided and cannot be recovered by a non-taxpayer. Higher-rate taxpayers must pay a further 22.5% of the gross dividend.

Investment income not taxable

Income from the following investments is free

of tax:

~ National Savings Certificates and Children's Bonus Bonds

~ Premium Bonds

~ TESSAs (until maturity)

~ ISAs and PEPs

~ Friendly Society savings schemes

~ employee share option schemes

~ enterprise investment schemes and venture capital trusts (EIS and VCT)

~ commercial forestry.*

Employees

Pay-as-you-earn (PAYE)

If you are in employment you are taxed under this system. Each employee is given a code number by the tax authorities each year, which the employer uses to calculate the tax to be deducted. The object is to spread the annual allowances evenly over the year.

* Take advantage of tax-efficient investments but remember to compare returns on all investments after tax and charges – and take account of risk!

Employers have tables from which they can read the weekly or monthly deduction to make, on a cumulative basis, and calculate the net pay accordingly. Code numbers are therefore based mainly on annual allowances, but will take into account other factors, too, such as taxable fringe benefits (see below).

If any of your circumstances alter during the year, you can notify your tax office and your code number may be changed.

Employees usually receive a weekly or monthly pay slip showing (among other things) tax deducted in the period and the cumulative tax deducted in the year to date. They must receive after the year-end a form – P60 – showing total pay for the year and total tax deducted.

Employees (including company directors and pensioners) with more complex tax affairs are required to complete self-assessment tax returns (see below).

If you leave your job you must be given a P45, which shows your code number, and a copy of it must be given to your new employer.

Students who work in the holidays and whose total income for the year is below the personal allowance can avoid PAYE. Get form P38S from your local tax office and submit it to your employer. (National Insurance deductions cannot be avoided.)

Taxable benefits-in-kind

Some fringe benefits are taxable and the employer is required to submit to the tax office, after the year-end, a form P11D in respect of each employee paid over £8,500 a year, listing the costs of all fringe benefits received. A copy has to be given to the employee (who might need it for completing self-assessment forms).

The relevant amounts are added to taxable income, so are in effect taxed at your highest rate.

Employers can obtain from the tax office a dispensation form showing expenses on the P11D in respect of certain tax-free fringe benefits.

For employees earning less than £8,500 a year, the taxable amount for benefits-in-kind is the value of the benefit to the employee rather than the cost to the employer. So, for example, the provision of a suit of clothes would be valued for tax at the second-hand value.

Tax-free benefits are dealt with in the next chapter. Taxable benefits include:

1. Company car or van. Many senior employees are allocated a company car and there is an annual taxable benefit of 35% of the car's list price when new.

    Where annual business mileage is 2,500 or more the benefit is reduced to 25% of the list price and, where it is 18,000 or more, to 15%. If the car is over four years old the benefit is reduced by one-quarter.

    There are further taxable benefits if the employer also pays for private fuel, based on engine size, as follows:

    | | Petrol | Diesel |
	£	£
1,400cc or less	1,930	2,460
1,401 to 2,000cc	2,460	2,460
2,001cc or more	3,620	3,620

Income Tax Rules 27

These amounts tend to change most years in the budget and will be increased by 20% above the inflation increases again next year. Also from 2002 it is proposed to change the basis of the tax to fuel emissions rather than mileage.

The taxable benefit for private use of a company van is currently £400 if it is under four years old, £350 if not.

2. Travelling expenses. Reimbursement of the cost of travel from home to the normal place of work is taxable. Otherwise travelling expenses are generally free of tax. There are lengthy rules.*

* Taxable fringe benefits, if of value to you, are better than nothing because your gain is the difference between what you pay in tax and the full cost if you paid for the benefit yourself.

Self-employed

There is a completely different method of taxing your income if you are self-employed. There is no PAYE, no code number and no weekly or monthly payment of tax. Instead you must complete self-assessment tax returns yourself (or employ an accountant to do it for you) and pay the tax in two annual instalments (see below).

The Inland Revenue has become tougher on ensuring that self-employment is genuine in the case of people who really have only one 'customer'. You need to be submitting invoices for work done and to be able to supply someone else if unable to perform the work yourself but, most of all, to have a number of clients.*

Self-assessment

The new self-assessment system is now in full operation. If you are in the system you receive in April the forms relating to the tax year just finished. The basic self-assessment tax return runs to eight pages and there are a number of supplementary pages covering specific circumstances.

With the return you receive a guide (the Tax Return Guide) showing how to fill in the forms and another guide (the Tax Calculation Guide) showing how to calculate your tax. You will be sent the supplementary pages thought to be applicable; you only have to fill

The advantage of being self-employed over being employed is one of cash flow – you pay the tax on your income later.

in those which are applicable, but if you think you should fill in any which have not been sent you must ask for them.

If you wish the tax office to calculate your tax liability you must submit the returns by 30 September. You will then receive a tax calculation. You will be notified in a statement of account sent to you in January of any amount due, which you are required to pay by 31 January. (Employees who only have a small liability will get it added to their code number for the following year.)

If you are prepared to calculate your own tax liability (perhaps because you are employing an accountant to do it) you have until the following 31 January to submit the return but it must be accompanied by the calculated payment.

You may be required (especially if self-employed) to make payments on account in respect of the current tax year. Such amounts are notified to you if you submit your return by 30 September or they form part of the calculation if you do it yourself. Half of these payments on account are due on 31 January in the current tax year and half on the 31 July following it.

It is a legal requirement to keep full records of your income, etc. and this is particularly important if you are self-employed.

It is best to send in tax returns well before the due date so that any problems can be sorted out in good time. If you send in returns late or fail to make payments when due, you may have to pay interest and/or fines.*

Summary points

★ Make sure you get your fair share of allowances and reliefs.

★ Are you entitled to any of the new tax credits?

★ Check your investment income to see whether you could profitably change to tax-efficient investments.

* The Inland Revenue has a self-assessment helpline – 0645 000 444 – and if you have a computer they will supply a free disk which helps you fill in the forms – ring 0645 000 404.

★ Remember that taxable fringe benefits may be better than nothing.

★ If you are self-employed make sure it is genuine so that you cannot be classified as an employee.

★ You can get help and advice from your local Tax Enquiry Centre. The address and telephone number will be in your local telephone directory under Inland Revenue. They also have leaflets and will post them to you.

2 Income Tax Planning

Now you know the rules, you can start planning to reduce your income tax bill.

In this chapter, six things that really matter:
~ Tax-free benefits-in-kind
~ Taxable benefits-in-kind
~ Spouses
~ Children
~ Loss-making businesses
~ Annual planning

Many employees receive benefits-in-kind. Some benefits are taxable; some are not. It pays to know which is which.

There are special provisions favourable to spouses but you do have to be married for some of them. These continue during separation but end on divorce. So far none are extended to single-sex partnerships.

Children are treated like adults for tax

purposes but there are restrictions on income from assets passed to them from their parents (but not anyone else, grandparents in particular).

There are ways of reducing your income tax liability by having a legitimate business which makes losses.

If you do nothing else, you should check your position shortly before the year end, to ensure you have made the most of your annual allowances and reliefs.

Is this you?

• I get some fringe benefits at work but do not know whether they are taxable or not.
• My employer has offered me the choice of a salary increase or a fringe benefit – which should I accept? • Bill and I are getting married later this year – will our tax position change? • Yippee, I'm pregnant! It's not my first consideration but what happens about tax? • Is there anything I should do taxwise before 5th April?

Tax-free benefits-in-kind

There are a few benefits which can be provided by an employer on a tax-free basis. Find out if any are provided by your employer. Can you persuade your employer to provide some?

The following benefits are tax free.*

Pension contributions

Company contributions to a company pension scheme do not involve you in any tax liability and there is no limit. If you have a personal pension, company contributions to it within the Inland Revenue limits (see Chapter 1) are also free of tax on you.

Loans

An employer can make a loan to an employee of up to £5,000 at no interest or at a low rate of interest. Above that amount an imputed rate of interest (currently 7.75%) is used by the Inland Revenue to calculate a taxable benefit.

Some employers, particularly in London, use this to provide loans for the purchase of

*There is another argument to use with your employer at your annual pay review – tax-free benefits are also free of National Insurance contributions for the employer.

annual season tickets by employees and this is useful for employees as they can get the benefit of lower annual rates without paying in advance – instead they pay by monthly deduction from their pay.

Another method of using this benefit is to combine it with the provision of a company car. Ownership of the car is shared between the employer and employee, so that a higher value vehicle can be acquired without adding to the taxable fringe benefit.

Loans can also help with the purchase of other goods, or house repairs or extensions.

Relocation costs

If your employer moves you to another area, you can receive reimbursement of relocation costs totalling up to £8,000 on a tax-free basis. Beyond that amount it becomes a taxable benefit.

Golden handshakes

Statutory redundancy pay is tax-free and if you receive additional compensation for termination of your employment, up to

£30,000 may be tax-free. There are complicated rules and in particular your contract of employment must not provide for pay in lieu of notice.

If your proposed compensation is in excess of the tax-free amount, it may be worth considering diverting some of it to buy additional pension, provided you do not exceed your Inland Revenue maximum contributions for the year.

Mobile phones

These are no longer taxable benefits where provided by the employer.

Taxable benefits-in-kind

Details of taxable benefits are given in Chapter 1.

They may still be of value despite being taxable. For example, although in recent years the tax charge for a company car has been increased, it can still be cheaper for you than paying all the costs of owning your own car.

This argument also applies to some tax-free

fringe benefits above the maximum permitted. For example paying tax on the imputed interest of an interest-free company loan is cheaper than paying interest at the market rate on a loan from elsewhere. Even assuming you could borrow at the imputed rate you only pay at your marginal rate of income tax and even if it is the top rate of 40% you are still saving 60% of the cost.

Mileage allowances above the authorised amounts are another area where the value exceeds the tax cost.*

Spouses

There are various ways that a married couple can minimise their joint tax liabilities.

The most important is to ensure as far as possible that both make full use of their personal allowances and lower tax rates. If you are both earning then it is likely that you both have earnings exceeding your personal allowance. However, if this is not the case then it would be advantageous to transfer income from one to the other, as follows:

* *It can pay you to try for employee benefits even if they are taxable.*

- ~ If you are both on the same marginal tax rate: transfer assets between you to take full advantage of both of your Capital Gains Tax annual exemptions.
- ~ If you are on different marginal tax rates: transfer enough income-earning assets from the one on the higher rate to bring the income of the one on the lower rate up to an amount which takes full advantage of the lower rate(s), i.e.:

Higher marginal rate	Maximum income of other
10%	£4,535
20%	£6,415
40%	£33,935

Notes:

- ~ The 22% rate does not apply to unearned income.
- ~ There is no tax advantage in tranferring income beyond the point at which similar marginal rates are reached.
- ~ Transfers of assets between spouses must be without 'strings' to be effective for tax

purposes.

~ The maximum income figures will be higher for those over 65 because of their higher personal allowances.

Self-employed

If one of you is self-employed, could the other receive pay from the business, perhaps by performing clerical tasks? Could the business be in joint ownership so that the profits are shared?

When one partner does not work

A common situation (though perhaps less so now than in the past) is where the husband is employed and the wife is a full-time housewife. If this is your situation, the only way of transferring income from the husband to the wife is by putting savings in her name, so that she receives all the income from it. Clearly there has to be trust between the two of you.

Money can be freely transferred. Shares or units can be transferred between spouses (but not between unmarried couples) without consideration (i.e. payment) although the transfer must be without reservation. All that is required is the preparation of a standard share transfer form, which requires completion on the reverse side to explain the transaction. The transfer must be stamped, but only at the minimum amount of 50p. Transfer forms can be obtained from any law stationer.*

The married couple's allowance is now only available to pensioners. It is normally received by the husband, but can be transferred to the wife. However, since the allowance is limited to 10%, this action would save tax only if the wife does pay income tax but the husband does not.

Children

Children are liable for income tax and are entitled to the personal allowance and the lower rates.

There is a limit to the amount of capital

---

* *Apart from the free transfer of shares, all these steps can be taken by an unmarried couple.*

which parents can transfer to their children. It applies to capital which earns more than £100 a year per child. If income from transferred capital exceeds that amount, it is treated as income of the parent and is taxed accordingly.

Since the limit only applies to capital transferred by parents, there is nothing to prevent grandparents (or anyone else) from transferring capital to their grandchildren, although the inheritance tax rules apply (see Chapter 5).

A former loophole whereby parents could transfer assets to a trust for the benefit of their children has been closed. Income from such assets will now be taxed as income of the parents.

Loss-making businesses

If you have an expensive hobby (a good example is yachting) you might be able to turn it into a loss-making business. The losses can be set against other taxable income, thus reducing tax liability.

Professional advice is required to ensure that the hobby can be treated as a business. For example, you will need to be trading in some way, such as buying and selling yachts, teaching sailing or offering holidays.*

Annual planning

Code number

If you are employed, in January/February each year you should receive your code number for the following tax year. Check it carefully. If you think it should be higher, then approach the tax office immediately. Otherwise you will pay more PAYE income tax each week/month than you need to.

You should receive a guide to understanding your tax code each year with your first PAYE coding notice. It explains in very clear language how your tax allowances and deductions are calculated.

Before the tax year-end

It is possible to go back up to six years in order to recover overpaid tax, but it is worth

There needs to be some means, or potential means, of earning income.

reviewing the situation before the end of each tax year (i.e. before 5 April) because the sooner you collect a recovery of tax the better.

Check whether there have been any changes in your personal position which can affect your tax liability.*

Summary points

★ Now you know which benefits are tax free, see if your employer might consider some instead of a pay rise if appropriate. Point out the National Insurance saving.

★ Taxable benefits can still be financially viable as you only pay the tax, not the full cost.

★ Can you transfer any tax liability to or from your spouse or partner to reduce your joint tax bill?

★ Are your children's personal tax allowances being used? Compare income on a pre-tax

Are there any allowances or reliefs you can claim which you have previously overlooked?

basis.

★ Can you set up a legimate loss-making business to get back some of your tax liability?

★ Review your tax position before the year-end.

3 National Insurance Contributions

It is a mistake to regard National Insurance Contributions as being like those to a pension fund. There is no fund.

In this chapter, four things that really matter:
- ~ Employee contributions class 1
- ~ Self-employed contributions (classes 2 and 4)
- ~ Voluntary contributions (class 3)
- ~ Planning

There is a tendency to look upon National Insurance Contributions (NICs) as contributions to a fund rather like pension contributions. This is wrong. There is no fund and there are no rights to future benefits as a result of NICs.

Some benefits depend on contributions having been paid but benefits tend to change each year in the budget and have often been cut back.

NICs are out of kilter with income tax, not only in respect of rates at different earnings levels but also regarding what is 'taxable' and what is 'tax-free'.

The current government is doing something about this anomaly. Some benefits have been changed into tax credits and some attempt is being made to match the levels at which rates change. For example, the earnings threshold for income tax allowances and NICs has been brought in line from April 2001.*

Is this you?

• I seem to pay contributions on only part of my earnings. I'm glad about that but how do I find out if it is still too much? • I am self-employed and understand my contributions are based on profits; how does it work? • I am a full-time housewife. What would it cost to get the full state basic pension? • Is there any way I can reduce my NICs?

---

* It makes sense to recognise these so-called 'contributions' as in effect another tax on income.

Employee contributions class 1

First it is necessary to explain the lower and upper earnings limits, which are adjusted each year. The current figures are:

~ lower earnings limit (LEL): £87 a week (£4,535 a year)

~ upper earnings limit (UEL): £575 a week (£29,900 a year).

Contributions of 10% are paid on earnings between the LEL and UEL.

There is one further complication. Members of contracted-out occupational pension schemes have the 10% rate reduced to 8.4%. (Note that personal pensions do not receive the reduction – instead the DSS makes an equivalent payment into the scheme.)

Contributions are deducted from pay by the employer, who also pays a contribution.

Reliefs from income tax (such as expenses at work, for example – see Chapter 1) are generally free of NICs too.*

* *As the threshold for employee NICs is the same as for income tax, both the 10% and 22% income tax rates for employees are effectively 10% higher (8.4% if you are in a contracted out company pension scheme).*

Self-employed contributions (classes 2 and 4)

Instead of LELs and UELs, there are LPLs and UPLs (lower and upper profits levels). The current figures are:

~ lower profits level (LPL): £4,535 a year

~ upper profits level (UPL): £29,900.

In addition there is a small earnings exemption, currently £3,955.

Contributions are only payable if profits exceed the small earnings exemption. Then they are:

~ £2 a week in respect of profits up to the LPL (class 2)

~ 7% on profits between the LPL and UPL (class 4).

If you are self-employed, you are responsible for paying your contributions.*

* *As the starting rate for self-employed NICs is the same as for income tax, both the 10% and 22% income tax rates for the self-employed are effectively 7% higher.*

Voluntary contributions (class 3)

Voluntary contributions exist to permit persons who otherwise would not contribute to get the full state basic pension or widow's benefits (which require contributions throughout most of your working life to achieve the maximum).

The voluntary contribution is currently a flat rate of £6.75 a week.

These contributions are not normally necessary if you are off sick or unemployed, as you get credit for the relevant period.

Planning

National Insurance contributions are paid on earnings, not unearned income. Consequently any replacement of earnings by unearned income reduces your National Insurance bill.

In the case of benefits-in-kind for employees, the tax-free benefits are generally free of NICs. Taxable benefits are also free of NICs except in the case of taxable travelling expenses.

However employers are required to pay

NICs in respect of all taxable benefits (these are called class 1A contributions).

The main limitation on fringe benefits is that they must neither be reimbursements nor convertible into cash. For example, a season ticket paid for by the employer is free of NICs, but if the ticket is bought by the employee who is then reimbursed by the employer, then NICs are payable.

Petrol for private use must by paid by company voucher or company credit card.

Examples of benefits convertible into cash are tradeable assets such as gold bullion and gemstones. Alcoholic liquor is also specifically made subject to NICs.

Other examples of fringe benefits free of NICs are board and lodging; clothing; gifts of tangible items (not money) in respect of long-service awards, birthday or retirement presents; luncheon vouchers; club membership fees; fees to professional bodies (if membership is a condition of employment); medical insurance; school fees.*

* *There is clearly an advantage in receiving fringe benefits instead of pay, if your income is below the upper earnings level.*

Summary points

★ If you are an employee, can you get your employer to substitute your next pay increase with tax-free benefits?

★ You can still have tax-free benefits if you are self-employed. Your profits will be reduced by the cost and you will save NICs as well as tax.

★ Should you or any of your family be paying voluntary National Insurance contributions to get benefits not otherwise available?

★ If you cannot get any tax-free benefits, how about taxable benefits? The problem is that, although you do not have to pay NICs on them, your employer does.

4 Capital Gains Tax

Capital gains tax (CGT) is payable on the sale not only of stocks and shares but also of a number of other things.

In this chapter, six things that really matter:
~ Taxable gains and losses
~ Indexation
~ Taper relief
~ Calculating the gain
~ Reliefs
~ Planning

Taxable sales include a second home (or even part of the first or main home if that part is let or used only for business), antiques, in fact anything other than household goods and personal effects up to an individual limit in value of £6,000.

Private motor vehicles are excluded.

There are also the following investment

exemptions:

- ~ gilt-edged stock
- ~ company debentures and loan stocks
- ~ ISAs and PEPs
- ~ permanent interest-bearing shares of building societies (PIBs)
- ~ enterprise investment schemes and venture capital trusts (EIS and VCT)
- ~ commercial forestry.

Only gains since 31 March 1982 are taxable. The market value on 31 March 1982 of any investment purchased earlier is taken as the cost for CGT purposes: many companies show the relevant figure in their annual report.

Is this you?

• I made some capital losses this year. Can I set them against gains? • How do I calculate indexed cost to reduce my CGT liability? • When does the new taper relief start to apply? • How do I calculate my CGT liability for the year? • Are there any reliefs I can set against my taxable gains? • Is there anything I should do before the year-end?

Taxable gains and losses

Capital losses are set off against capital gains in the same tax year and after that there is an annual exemption, currently £7,500. As a result, few people pay capital gains tax.

If the net result of a year's transactions before the annual exemption is a loss, it can be carried forward to succeeding years. The annual exemption cannot be carried forward, but can be applied to the net gains for a year before using any loss brought forward from the previous year which, if not used in the current year, can be carried forward to the following year.

Losses brought forward from the previous year can be partly used in the current year, with the balance remaining being carried forward to the following year.

Keeping records

In order to be able to calculate taxable gains on shares it is necessary to keep full records of each transaction, the minimum being:

~ date
~ type of transaction (purchase or sale)
~ description of item
~ number of units
~ charges incurred
~ transaction value.*

Indexation

For purchases before April 1998 the cost can be indexed, that is adjusted by the cumulative rate of inflation (RPI) between purchase and April 1998. However, indexation cannot be taken beyond break-even, i.e. it cannot be used to create or increase a loss.

The Inland Revenue issues a table of the capital gains tax indexation allowances each month and the final table needed, that for April 1998, is included in Inland Revenue leaflet CGT1. (It would be a good idea to

* *There are computer systems which make keeping records easy, but it is very important to maintain a regular back-up file. Either way, keep all your original transaction forms as a back-up.*

prepare the indexation of holdings bought before 5 April 1998 in advance of future sales.)

Multiple dealings

Where there are multiple dealings in a share, such as successive purchases, taking up a rights issue or taking shares instead of a cash dividend, then calculating the indexation is complicated.

Bonus and rights issues are simple because for CGT purposes they are not treated as new issues, so the date of acquisition of the original shares applies. However, taking shares for a cash dividend is treated as a new acquisition on the date the new shares are issued.

The best way of dealing with multiple transactions is to index the original cost up to the date of the next transaction, add the cost of that, then index the total until the date of the next transaction and so on to April 1998. The indexation table can be used in this way.

Matching purchases and sales of shares

Shares sold are identified in the following order:
1. Purchases on same day as sale.
2. Purchases within 30 days of sale.
3. Purchases since 5 April 1998, the most recent first.
4. Purchases between 6 April 1982 and 5 April 1998.†‡
5. Purchases between 6 April 1965 and 5 April 1982.†
6. Purchases before 6 April 1965.†

† Purchases between these dates are 'pooled' to arrive at an average cost per share. Indexation will need to be calculated separately for each pool.

‡ Purchases between 17 March and 5 April 1998 should be segregated because they do not get the extra year for taper relief (see below).

Taper relief

From April 1998 indexation was replaced by

taper relief. It only applies to shares held for at least three complete years. The percentage of the gain chargeable reduces to 95% after the third complete year and by a further 5% for each successive year, to a minimum of 60% after ten complete years.

More favourable taper relief applies to the sale of assets used in your business (if you have one) whether as a sole trader or as a partner, shares in a company where you are an employee, shares in unquoted and AIM quoted companies and property rented out to an unquoted trading company.

Before 6 April 2000, this only applied to business assets and shares in a company where you held 25% of the voting rights or 5% if you were a full-time director or employee, including unquoted and AIM-quoted, non-trading and venture capital companies.

Where assets qualify only from 6 April 2000, the gain before taper relief on sale of assets owned on that date will have to be apportioned in accordance with the length of time the assets were owned as a business and non-business asset.

Taper relief reduces the amount of an individual gain the longer an asset is held. The percentage taper for each category, together with the equivalent tax rate, is:

No. of complete years after 5.4.98 for which asset held	Gains on non-business assets		Gains on business assets	
	Percentage of gain chargeable	*Equivalent tax rates for higher rate/basic rate taxpayer*	*Percentage of gain chargeable*	*Equivalent tax rates for higher rate/basic rate taxpayer*
0	100	40 / 22.00	100	40/22
1	100	40 / 22.00	87.5	35/19.25
2	100	40 / 22.00	75	30/16.5
3	95	38 / 20.9	50	20/11
4	90	36 / 19.8	25	10/5.5
5	85	34 / 18.7		
6	80	32 / 17.6		
7	75	30 / 16.5		
8	70	28 / 15.4		
9	65	26 / 14.3		
10 or more	60	24 / 13.2		

An extra year is added to the taper relief score for all non-business assets held on 17 March 1998, so for such assets the three-year period is already up and taper relief can be applied.

Calculating the gain

The steps involved in calculating the annual chargeable gain are as follows:

1 Calculate the indexed cost to 5 April 1998 (if not already done).

2 Calculate the gain or loss after indexation on each sale. (Indexation cannot be used to create or increase a loss.)

3 List all the gains in ascending order of complete years held after 5 April 1998 (remember that an extra year is added to all holdings on 17 March 1998).

4 Set any losses in the current year against the individual gains, starting with those held for the least number of years (because this produces the lowest tax charge).

5 Apportion any gain on shares which were held on 6 April 2000 and which then became business assets, in proportion to

the time held as a business and non-business asset.

6 Apply taper relief as appropriate to each remaining gain.

7 Total the net gains for the year, after indexation and taper relief, and deduct the annual exempt amount (currently £7,500), to arrive at the net chargeable gain for the year.

8 If you have any losses brought forward from the previous year, they are used to reduce the net chargeable gain, but in order to do this you have to go back to 4 above, as losses must be applied before taper relief. But leave sufficient gains after taper relief to utilise the full annual exempt amount.*

See Appendix B for an example of a taxable capital gain calculation.

The net chargeable gain for the year is added to your income and is taxed at 10% if any falls within the personal allowance or the 10% band, at 20% for any within the basic rate band (not 22% as for income) and 40% thereafter. CGT liability cannot be set against personal allowances.

Reliefs

Private residence relief

Subject to certain exceptions, you do not pay CGT on any gain you make when you sell your home. Nor, on the other hand, can you set off any loss against gains made elsewhere.

If you have a large property, for example if your grounds are larger than half a hectare (about one-and-a-quarter acres), or if part is used exclusively for a trade or business, the relief may be restricted.

There may also be restrictions if you have not occupied the property during the whole period of ownership, or if some or all of it has been let as residential accommodation for part of the time.

If you take in lodgers, under the rent-a-room scheme for example (see Chapter 1), no CGT is payable if they are treated as members of your family, sharing your living room and eating with you. If not, CGT will be payable on a proportional basis, taking account of how much of your home you let and the length of time for which you let it.

If you have two or more residences, only one can be treated as your main residence at a time but you can nominate which one for any period, subject to a time limit.

Relief is also available on disposal of a residence acquired before 6 April 1988 for occupation by a dependent relative.

For more information on these complicated rules see Inland Revenue Helpsheet IR283, *Private Residence Relief*.

Re-investment relief

Chargeable gains on disposals can be deferred indefinitely if the amounts realised are reinvested in new share issues from qualifying companies under the Enterprise Investment Scheme.

Retirement relief

This is available to business people from the age of 50. You must be disposing of the whole or part of your business, including your share in a partnership, or shares in a company where you have worked full-time as a director or manager and own at least 5% of the voting rights.

The relief is being phased out, following the introduction of taper relief for business assets (see above)

The figures are:

	100% relief on gains up to	*50% relief on gains between*
2001/2002	£100,000	£100,001 to £400,000
2002/2003	£50,000	£50,001 to £200,000*

CGT on death

CGT is not payable on assets held by the deceased at the date of death; instead the full amount goes to increase the value of the estate for inheritance tax purposes. The assets are taken over by the executors at their market value on the date of death.

If assets are transferred to beneficiaries of the estate, the base cost for CGT purposes is

* *Retirement relief for business people may be more advantageous than taper relief which replaces it, so any business person over 50 should take advantage of it as soon as possible.*

the market value on date of death.

If the executors realise any of the assets then a CGT liability arises. The normal annual exemption is available in the year of death and for two following years but not thereafter. The rate of tax charged is the basic income tax rate (currently 22%).

Planning

Planning for capital gains tax is mainly a matter of ensuring you make use of your annual tax-free allowance of £7,500, because if it is not used by the year-end it is lost.

You should keep a running record of your sales during each financial year (starting 6 April), with a note of the gain or loss, after adjusting for indexation. Losses before indexation can of course be deducted from gains.

Check on the cumulative position by the beginning of February, taking account of any losses in the year and the effect of taper relief.

If you have a substantial amount of your

annual allowance still available, then take a look at the unrealised gains in your portfolio and consider whether to realise any of them.*

Bed-and-breakfasting

Before 17 March 1998 any unused annual allowance could be applied to unrealised gains before the end of the tax year, by selling the shares one day and buying them back the next (known as bed-and-breakfasting). This has now been stopped by introducing a 30-day interval between selling and buying back, otherwise the two transactions will be ignored for CGT purposes.

It is of course possible to take the risk of being out of the market for 30 days.

Other alternatives are:

~ If you are married (or there is anyone else you have joint funds with) you can sell and your spouse/joint fundholder buy back (or vice-versa), although there is a view that too many such transactions may give rise to a query from the Inland Revenue

~ You can buy a similar share (eg BP for

* *Without proper planning just before the year end, it is possible to lose some of your annual allowance or to pay tax you could have deferred.*

Shell) or your best choice of new investment, perhaps coming back to the share sold in another sell-and-buy transaction in 30 days.

~ If you have not used all your current year's ISA allowance or have uninvested amounts in a PEP, then you can 'bed-and-ISA' or 'bed-and-PEP', that is buy back into an ISA or PEP.

In all these alternatives the sale and buy-back can be done simultaneously, so there is no risk of overnight adverse price movement, as there was with bed-and-breakfasting.

The disadvantage is that costs of both selling and buying (including stamp duty) are incurred, although some stockbrokers will forgo some or all of their commission on the second transaction. Also you lose the difference between the buying and selling prices.

Summary points

★ Before you sell something, whether at a

gain or a loss, you need to know whether it is subject to CGT.

★ If you held investments before 6 April 1998, you should calculate the indexation on each and add it to your records – it will be useful when year-end planning.

★ Make sure you apply taper relief to the gains from assets you held longest, to get the most benefit from it.

★ Calculate the taxable gain (or loss) on each asset you sell as you go along, to simplify year-end planning.

★ Have you made the most of any reliefs available to you?

★ When it comes to the year-end and you still have some of the annual exempt amount (currently £7,500) unused, consider the alternative ways of realising some unrealised gains.

5 Inheritance Tax

Inheritance tax (IHT) is normally payable on death but can be partly payable earlier. It is also sometimes called a voluntary tax, because there are so many ways of avoiding it but they are not straightforward.

In this chapter, six things that really matter:
- ~ Exempt lifetime transfers
- ~ Potentially exempt and immediately chargeable transfers and taper relief
- ~ Investments free of IHT
- ~ Calculating the inheritance tax payable
- ~ Planning
- ~ Deeds of variation

The exempt amount, or threshold, for IHT is currently £242,000. Whilst this sounds a high figure, think of the value of your house.

Tax is payable on the estate above the threshold at the flat rate of 40%. Interest on the tax due is payable if it has not been paid within six months of the date of death.

The problem with IHT payable on death is that it must be paid before probate is granted, but without probate the executors of the will may not be able to get hold of the cash, so may have to borrow. (Probate is official permission to executors to carry out the terms of the will. In the absence of a will it is necessary to obtain letters of administration – the same problem arises.)*

In addition to releasing cash on deposit for funeral expenses and the probate fee, a bank may be prepared to release it before probate for paying IHT and likewise stockbrokers may release equities held in nominee accounts.

Certain investments which include life cover, such as with-profits bonds, although subject to IHT, can be written into trust so that they pass directly to your heirs and can then be realised to meet at least some of the tax bill.

If the estate includes property, then a proportion of IHT payable equal to the proportion of the property to the total estate can be deferred.

Is this you?

• I would like to give some money to my children but will IHT be payable on it? • I have heard that if I live for at least seven years after giving some money away, IHT will not be payable on it. But what happens if I die just before the seven years are up? • I am sorting out my father's estate. How do I work out how much IHT is payable? • Would it be advantageous to give some money away now rather than waiting until I die? • My husband died recently and left everything to me, but I would like some to go to our children. Is there anything I can do about it?

Exempt lifetime transfers

The following lifetime transfers are exempt from IHT:

~ Transfers between spouses.

~ £3,000 payment from capital (this is an annual exemption which can be carried forward one year but no longer).

- ~ Small gifts not exceeding £250 each, without limit in number, but only if you have not also given a recipient any of the other exempt gifts in the same year.

- ~ A series of regular gifts from surplus income; but there must be no reduction in capital nor in the standard of living of the donor (the taxpayer must be able to show that these requirements are met).

- ~ Gifts relating to marriage:
    - up to £5,000 from each parent
    - up to £2,500 to a direct descendant (eg a grandchild)
    - up to £1,000 to anyone else.

- ~ Gifts for maintenance of the family (this applies to spouses, and children up to age 18 or until completion of full-time education).

- ~ Gifts to charities, museums and political parties.

- ~ Gifts of investments in unquoted securities, including investments in the alternative investment market (AIM), which have been held for more than two years.

You can make gifts to the same person under any of the above headings in the same year without incurring IHT, except the small gifts of £250 each. So for example you can give your child a wedding gift of £5,000 plus £3,000 (plus another £3,000 if you did not use it last year).

Another interesting use of exempt amounts is that contributions can be made to stakeholder pensions for someone else – for your children or even your grandchildren (there is no minimum age).*

Potentially exempt and immediately chargeable transfers and taper relief

Potentially exempt transfers (PETs)

These are lifetime gifts to individuals or certain trusts which are not otherwise exempt. If the donor lives for seven years after the gift is made no IHT is payable, but if the donor dies within the seven years then the PET is included in the estate for IHT purposes.

Lifetime transfers should be documented, so that there are no arguments about the IHT position after your death.

Immediately chargeable transfers (ICTs)

Lifetime gifts to companies or discretionary trusts which are not otherwise exempt are immediately chargeable transfers. IHT is immediately payable at half the rate (20%) on any amount exceeding the threshold on a cumulative basis with any other ICTs within the last seven years.

If death occurs within seven years, then the ICT is included in the estate and further tax may be payable but tax already paid cannot be recovered.

Taper relief

When PETs and ICTs within seven years of death are included in an estate, they are first set against the threshold in chronological order. If their total exceeds the threshold then the relevant donees (the recipients of the gifts), not the estate, are responsible for paying the IHT on them.

If the period since the excess amounts were paid is more than three years, then taper relief applies. Tax on the relevant amounts is reduced to 80% of the full charge (i.e. 32% tax) in the fourth year, 60% of it (24%) in the fifth year, 40% (16%) in the sixth and 20% (8%) in the seventh year.

In the case of ICTs, tax already paid is deducted from the tax due, but cannot be used to create a refund.

Taper relief is sometimes misunderstood. It does not apply to the full amount of PETs and ICTs made within the seven years before death, but only to amounts exceeding the threshold and before any legacies on death.*

Investments free of IHT

Provided you have invested for at least two years, the following are exempt:

~ investments in AIM and unquoted shares

~ commercial forestry

~ assets connected to Lloyds of London.

All other investments are subject to IHT, including ISAs., PEPs and TESSAs

See Appendix C for an example of how ICTs, PETs and taper relief work.

Calculating the inheritance tax payable

The following steps should be followed:

1 Identify everything to be included in the estate.

2 Delete any items which are exempt (eg whatever is willed to the spouse).

3 Sort into chronological order any gifts made within seven years of the date of death which are not exempt (i.e. ICTs and PETs) and add to the estate.

4 Value all items in the estate and total.

5 Deduct allowable expenses, such as debts of the deceased and 'reasonable' funeral costs.

6 This gives the total chargeable amount.

7 Set any ICTs and PETs against the threshold on the date of death, until they

or it are used up.

8 If any threshold is left after deducting ICTs and PETs, deduct it from the chargeable amount relating to the rest of the estate. Tax is payable on the balance remaining.

9 If any ICTs and/or PETs are left after using up the threshold:

   i   Calculate whether taper relief applies and reduce the tax payable on them accordingly.

   ii If any ICTs are included in 9.1, deduct the tax already paid from the net amount payable after taper relief, but not so as to create a negative figure.

   iii Calculate the tax payable on the rest of the estate and add to the net amounts arising from 9.i and 9.ii to give the total tax payable.*

If the estate includes any property, calculate its proportion to the total estate and apply that to the tax payable to calculate how much can be deferred.

Planning

Although transfers between husband and wife are exempt, if your joint estate (which includes your home) is significantly in excess of the threshold then instead of each leaving everything to the other, it would be sensible to find some way of utilising the exempt amount on the first death in order to avoid or reduce the IHT liability on the second death.

The trouble is that most married couples need their assets to live on during their lifetime, or at least during the remaining life of the survivor of the two, so they cannot afford to give any of it away.

There are a number of ways of taking action without impoverishing yourselves.

Inclusion in the will

The following routes require inclusion in the will and do not come into operation until the first death:

The family home
If this is owned jointly then it passes to the survivor without forming part of the estate.

However, if it is owned as tenants-in-common (each spouse owns half), then half will form part of the estate of each spouse and part or all of that half can be willed to the children.

A further possible advantage of part ownership by the family after the first death is that if the survivor has to go into long-term care, then that part of the value is excluded from the means test.

Arrangements can be made for the survivor to prevent sale of the house during his or her lifetime, but careful legal drafting is required in order to avoid the arrangement being treated as a gift-with-reservation, which would mean it stays in the estate of the survivor.

Arrangements can also be made for ownership to revert to a joint basis after the first death, which may be better protection for the survivor and for the children, as the part owned by the survivor will be outside that person's estate when they die.

However, on either basis of ownership, the children have the right to joint occupation, so disputes can arise. Also the death or divorce of one of the children can present problems. Consequently this course of action needs careful consideration and many experts advise against it.*

Trusts
There are a number of different forms of trusts which can be set up to receive a capital sum from your estate within the IHT threshold. The right one for you depends on whether the surviving spouse will need income from the capital amount or at least access to it in case of need. One form of trust loans the money or assets back to the surviving spouse, to use as he or she likes, the loan being repayable on the second death.

Outside the will

The following are outside the will and take effect immediately:

~ **Loan for investment.** This device only gives away the growth content of capital. A trust is set up and loans are made to it

---

* *Another disadvantage is that the children may be subject to capital gains tax on any rise in the value of their share after probate, when the property is finally sold.*

within the threshold, which are then invested. Up to 5% of the loans can be repaid each year, thus providing income. There is currently some doubt about whether the annual repayments are free of tax - this needs sorting out before proceeding.

~ **Back-to-back plan.** An annuity is purchased, part of the income being used to buy life assurance to pass the capital to the children and part to provide income. It is only appropriate if you are over 70, because below that age the returns on annuities are inadequate.

~ **Split-capital investment trust.** This is an investment where there are income shares and capital shares. The idea is that you invest half the money in each, up to the threshold, keep the income shares (effectively giving you the same income as before) and pass the capital shares (with the potential future growth) to your children.

Getting advice

All the above routes require the help of a solicitor with experience in IHT, to ensure that the tax is avoided.*

Many investment advisers (especially those who are tied to a provider) offer forms of investment which fall into one or other of the trusts outlined above. Usually they require investment of all the sums involved in one place, thus earning the adviser substantial commission.

However it may not be convenient to produce the cash, as existing investments may have to be sold, at a cost and possibly also at the wrong time. Furthermore, there is more risk in having all your investments in one vehicle. It may not be necessary to take such action to achieve the desired result.

Gifts before or on the first death

For those who can afford to part with their capital and income before or on the first death, then more direct action can be taken.

Obviously each partner can give or will to

You might consider the loan trust to be the best choice, because it has the minimum effect on the surviving spouse.

their children assets up to the threshold. If these are appreciating assets, so much the better. A trust can be used to benefit grandchildren as well or even to skip a generation, if that is appropriate. With the seven-year rule such gifts can be repeated every seven years.

In the case of investments in AIM or unquoted stocks, the transfer free of IHT can be made after only two years' ownership.

Another way is to take out life assurance, with the beneficiaries named as recipients of the benefit. This is called being 'written into trust' and most life assurance companies will provide the necessary documentation, although some make a charge. (If you have existing life assurance that you wish to have treated this way, unfortunately the seven-year rule applies, but not if it is done at the commencement of the policy.)

Term assurance would be suitable for PETs and/or ICTs, if you have a potential liability over the seven years before they fall out of the tax net, as it is cheaper. Reducing-balance term assurance (under which the benefit reduces with the lapse of time) is worth considering in the case of PETs and/or ICTs exceeding the threshold and potentially covered by taper relief, as it is cheaper still.

If you have a pension which pays a lump sum if you die, ensure that it goes directly to your beneficiaries, thus bypassing your estate and any IHT liability.*

Deeds of variation

A will can be varied for up to two years after a death, with the agreement of all the beneficiaries who would be adversely affected. This can be done even if there is no will. You need to get a solicitor to prepare a deed of variation. Such a change could affect the IHT payable on the estate, as the variation dates back to the date of death. For example where a widow, instead of receiving all the estate, wishes some to go to her children, and the amount diverted exceeds the threshold, then IHT would be payable on the excess amount. (But she might in that case restrict the change to the threshold and deal

---

* The Chancellor's threat to tackle tax avoidance may stop some of these ideas and such action might be retrospective to a scheme in a will where the Testator (the person who made the will) is still alive.

with the balance as a PET from her, which would reduce or avoid tax if she were to live long enough.)

It is necessary for all beneficiaries who would be adversely affected to agree to the variation but not those unaffected. For example if a fixed sum is left to a charity and the balance of the estate to a spouse then the charity would not need to agree.

Summary points

★ If you can afford to give some money to your children now, make sure it falls within the exempt amount (currently £242,000).

★ Avoid making immediately chargeable transfers, as some IHT is payable at that point; potentially exempt transfers are much more effective.

★ You need to know how IHT is calculated in order to take steps to avoid it.

- ★ If the joint estate of you and your spouse is likely to exceed the exempt amount, find some way of utilising it on the first death.

- ★ If one of your parents dies and the Will is unsatisfactory for IHT purposes, consider a deed of variation.

Appendix A
Example of the Extra Age and Married Couples' Allowances for Pensioners

Alan is 67 and retired. Ann, his wife, is 64 and still working.

Their income is as follows:

	Alan	Ann
	£	£
State retirement pension	3,770	–
Personal pension annuity	10,760	–
Pay	–	6,220
Taxable savings income	1,600	1,600
	16,130	7,820

and their tax allowances:

Personal	5,990	4,535
Married couples' £5,365 at 10%	536	
	6,526	

Alan's income is below the limit of £17,600 for higher age and married couples' allowances.

If his income were £2,000 higher, he would

be over the limit by £530 and the extra amount of personal allowance would be cut back by £1 for every £2 over, i.e. by half of £530 = £265.

If his income was even higher the cut-back would continue until his personal allowance was reduced to the under-65 amount of £4,535. The extra allowance is £5,990 − £4,535 = £1,455, so Alan's income could exceed the limit by twice that, i.e. £2,910, before losing all the extra.

But then the cut-back starts to apply to the married couples' allowance (MCA). The extra MCA is £5,365 − £2,070 = £3,295, so Alan's income could go up by a further amount of twice that, i.e. £6,590, before losing all the extra MCA too.

Would it make a difference to transfer some of the savings income to Ann? No, not at present, because her marginal rate is 22%, the same as Alan's.

If Ann's marginal rate was only 10% then it would be worth transferring income to her to use up the balance of the 10% band.

If Alan's income was higher so that his

extra personal allowance was being cut back, then it would be worth transferring income to Ann (even though both are on a marginal rate of 22%), to reduce the cut-back. Taking the example of a cut-back of £530, then transferring savings income of that amount to Ann would eliminate the cut-back and save £116.60 tax (22% of £530).

Appendix B
Example of a Taxable Capital Gains Calculation on Shares

Transaction record

		Monthly CGTI*
17.1.95	Bought 1,000 shares at 210p each commission £20, stamp duty £10	0.114
28.6.96	Bonus issue of 1 new share for each existing share held	0.063
4.10.97	Rights issue of 1 for 2 at 200p	0.019
11.2.98	Scrip dividend taken up of 100 shares at 220p each	0.014
12.4.99	Sold 1,000 shares for 271p each commission £20	

*Index numbers are taken from the monthly table of capital gains tax indexation allowances for April 1998, issued by the Inland Revenue and published in investment and tax magazines.

Calculation

Original cost £2,100 + £20 + £10 = £2,130

The bonus issue is ignored as no cost is involved, but the number of shares doubles to 2,000

Index to Oct. 97: 0.114 - 0.019 = 0.095

	£
£2,130 × 1.095 =	2,332
Add: rights issue cost 1,000 × £2 =	2,000
Indexed cost of 3,000 shares	4,332

Index to Feb. 98: 0.019 - 0.014 = 0.005

	£
£4,332 × 1.005 =	4,353
Add: scrip dividend cost 100 × £2.20 =	220
Indexed cost of 3,100 shares	4,573

Indexed cost to April 98: £4,573 × 1.014 = £4,637

	£
Indexed cost of 1,000 shares = £4,637 × 1,000/3,100 =	1,495
Net sale proceeds 1,000 × £2.71 − £20 =	2,690
Taxable gain	1,195

*April 1998 is the final month for indexation. There is no taper relief yet in this case.

Appendix C
Example of How Immediately Chargeable Transfers, Potentially Exempt Transfers and IHT Taper Relief Work

Mary, a rich widow, put £150,000 into a discretionary trust for her family, on 31.12.94. This was an ICT (immediately chargeable transfer) but as this was her first transfer and was within the threshold then – also £150,000 – no inheritance tax was payable.

Two years later she gave assets worth £50,000 each to her son and daughter. These were PETs (potentially exempt transfers) so no tax was payable.

Mary died on 1.3.98. (The threshold had by then gone up to £215,000.)

All the above transfers fall into the seven-year period before her death and so are liable for tax. They are set against the threshold in chronological order, as follows:

Threshold	£215,000
31.12.94 ICT	£150,000
Balance	£65,000
31.12.96 PETs	£100,000
Taxable PETs	£35,000

(The rest of the estate is ignored for the purpose of this example.)

As less than three years have passed, taper relief does not apply.

However, if Mary had made the two PETs earlier, say between 1.1.95 and 28.2.95, three years would have passed, so the tax payable on the £35,000 would have been reduced by taper relief to 80% of 40%, i.e. to 32%, saving 8% of £35,000.

What if the £100,000 on 31.12.96 had also been paid into the discretionary trust? The threshold had by then increased to £200,000 but tax would have been immediately payable, as follows:

Total payments within 7 years	£250,000
Threshold	£200,000
Taxable ICT	£50,000

Tax at half the death rate, i.e. 20% = £10,000

On Mary's death, when the threshold had gone up to £215,000, a further 20% would have been payable on £250,000 − £215,000 = £35,000 i.e. £7,000.

If Mary had lived another two years, say (and assuming no further change in the threshold), then the tax payable would have been reduced by taper relief to 80% of 40%, i.e. 32%. The 20% already paid would be deducted, leaving 12% to pay on the £35,000, i.e. £4,200.

If she had lived a further four years (and still assuming no change in the threshold), no extra tax would have been payable, as taper relief would have reduced the tax payable to 40% of 40% i.e. 16% and, as 20% would already have been paid, no further tax would be payable. But refunds are not permitted, so there would be no recovery of the 4% overpayment.